T Y P E

SIX

The Loyalist, Skeptic, Guardian

Brimming with creative inspiration, how-to projects, and useful information to enrich your everyday life, quarto.com is a favorite destination for those pursuing their interests and passions.

© 2022 Quarto Publishing Group USA Inc.
Text © 2022 Carver and Green

First Published in 2022 by Fair Winds Press, an imprint of The Quarto Group,
100 Cummings Center, Suite 265-D, Beverly, MA 01915, USA.
T (978) 282-9590 F (978) 283-2742 Quarto.com

Fair Winds Press titles are also available at discount for retail, wholesale, promotional, and bulk purchase. For details, contact the Special Sales Manager by email at specialsales@quarto.com or by mail at The Quarto Group, Attn: Special Sales Manager, 100 Cummings Center, Suite 265-D, Beverly, MA 01915, USA.

ISBN: 978-0-7603-7781-9

Cover Image and Illustration: Liz Carver
Page Layout: Megan Jones Design

ENNEATYPE 6
THE LOYALIST, SKEPTIC, GUARDIAN

An Interactive Workbook

Liz Carver and Josh Green

FAIR WINDS

CONTENTS

Introduction 9

PART I:
Being a Type SIX 11

PART II:
Digging Deeper
as a Type SIX 37

PART III:
Relationships
as a Type SIX 59

PART IV:
The Way Forward
as a Type SIX 71

About the Authors 93

Index 94

INTRODUCTION

Welcome to the type SIX enneaguide! This book is designed to help you ask deeper questions of yourself, your motivations, your coping strategies, and more. We always say that knowing your type is just the first step; after that, the real work begins. In other words, knowing your type is information; digging deeper to ask the harder questions is the start of transformation.

You can go through this enneaguide at whatever pace suits you best. Some questions will be easy for you to answer off the top of your head. Others will require you to sit and think for a minute. Some may even require you to sit with them for a few days or more. Sometimes, you'll be prompted to do something in real life and then reflect on that experience. The goal isn't to simply finish this book and move on to the next thing. Rather, this book should be a tool to help you understand yourself better in relation to the world around you so you can live a fuller, more integrated life.

This guide is for you, beloved SIX. We know that you won't identify with every aspect of SIX-ness, and that's okay. Feel free to invite loved ones who know you on this journey with you! They may be able to help you see things that you have a hard time seeing for yourself. Remember that a healthier and more self-aware you is a gift to everyone in your life. It is our hope that, through these lessons and prompts, you will find pathways for growth out of the box called SIX.

— Liz and Josh

PART I

BEING A TYPE SIX

In this section, we'll review some of the aspects of being a type SIX on a broad level so you can refamiliarize yourself with some of the SIX language and what SIXes are like in general. There will be aspects that you identify with strongly, and there may be aspects that you don't identify with at all. Both are completely fine. The point isn't that we (Liz and Josh) completely understand you, but that you have the space to understand yourself and identify why you are the way that you are.

MOTIVATION

SIXes are generally motivated by safety and security, both for themselves and for the people they love. They want to create environments where their needs can be met, where unpredictability or danger is mitigated, and where they trust the people around them. SIXes want to be prepared for any situation that may arise; they are the ones who always travel with snacks and a first aid kit, who have emergency escape routes planned at every public place, who know what to do in the event of a bear attack, and generally have you covered. They can find their safety and security in other people, so they are very protective of and loyal to people in their circle.

Below the surface, SIXes strive for security because at some level, they believe the world to be an unsafe place. They need to look out for themselves, because they believe that nobody else will look out for them. They surround themselves with trusted people as a way of making human safety nets. SIXes rely on their loved ones for the stability and security they can't find within themselves. Their rationale is often that, while the world is unpredictable, if they can surround themselves with people and routines that they know and understand, their little corner of it will be safe.

➤ How does this motivation resonate with you?

_____

_____

_____

_____

_____

_____

_____

➤ Are there aspects that you feel may be true for most SIXes but aren't true for you?

_____

_____

_____

_____

_____

_____

_____

➤ How does this motivation feed your own ego? How does it actually help you? How does it actually help others?

_____

_____

_____

_____

_____

_____

➤ Do you find it easy to say or claim what motivates you? If so, what else is motivating to you? If not, why do you have a hard time claiming these things?

_____

_____

_____

_____

_____

_____

_____

THE SHADOW SIDE

Just as each type has a great gift to give to the world, each type also has their shadow side: the parts of their type of which they're not proudest. The shadow side is what we need to root out, unlearn, and grow beyond. Also called the core vice, or "deadly sin," the shadow side for SIXes is fear. Fear, uncertainty, and anxiety that things may go wrong is a constant undercurrent that dictates much of the behavior of SIXes. Their way of coping with fear is by always diving headfirst into the worst-case scenario so they can be as prepared as possible, trying to get ahead of their fear before it's realized. Their general posture toward new people can be suspicion or distrust, assuming the person may not have their best interests in mind. When it comes to being loved and accepted, SIXes may settle for security and "knowing what they're getting" rather than holding out for what they actually want or deserve.

➤ How would you describe your shadow side in your own words?

_____

_____

_____

_____

_____

_____

_____

➤ How does fear show up for you?

_____

_____

_____

_____

_____

_____

_____

_____

_____

➤ How does fear manifest in your body? In your mind? In your soul?

_____

_____

_____

_____

_____

_____

_____

➤ Describe a time when you settled for security rather than being truly loved or desired. What did you learn from that? In what ways did the old habits stay the same after that?

_____

_____

_____

_____

_____

_____

_____

➤ If you were to strive for risky hopes and dreams rather than simply being safe, what would be the cost? How would it serve you?

_____

_____

_____

_____

_____

➤ Describe a time when you did the very thing that scared you because you knew that it was right. What was that experience like, and who was involved? What did you learn from that? How did you alter your behavior or mindset as a result of that experience?

_____

_____

_____

_____

_____

_____

_____

➤ Do you believe the lie that your constant vigilance is the only thing protecting you and your loved ones? What is keeping you bound to this lie? When have you felt released from this lie?

_____

_____

_____

_____

_____

_____

_____

_____

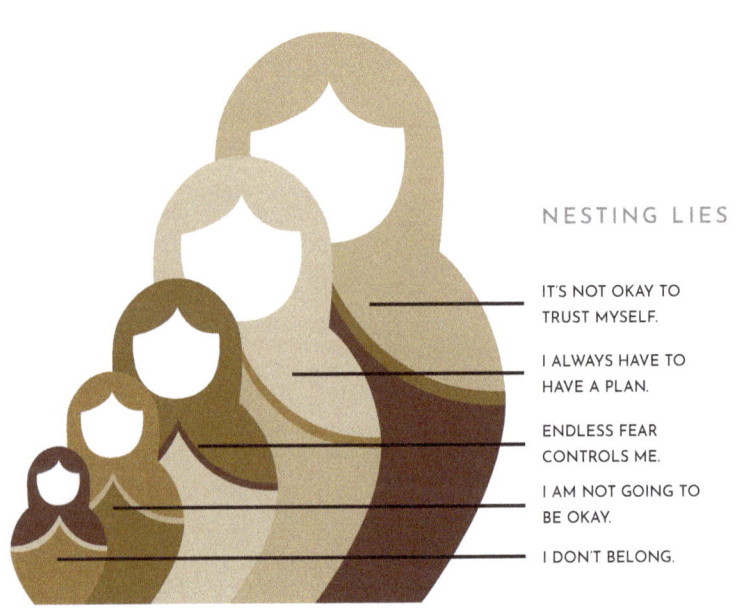

NESTING LIES

IT'S NOT OKAY TO TRUST MYSELF.

I ALWAYS HAVE TO HAVE A PLAN.

ENDLESS FEAR CONTROLS ME.

I AM NOT GOING TO BE OKAY.

I DON'T BELONG.

INTEGRATION AND DISINTEGRATION

When we move toward different types, whether in integration or disintegration, it's because we need something from that type that we can't get on our own. When SIXes are in moments or seasons of disintegration, they move toward THREE and take on some THREE characteristics. They can become more concerned with their image and less concerned with the safety and well-being of the people around them. Their usual tendency to think through everything and make careful decisions gives way a bit, toward impulsivity and reactivity to their surroundings. SIXes in disintegration can succumb to their insecurities and begin projecting them on everyone else, which can take the form of unhealthy competitiveness or unfair comparisons. They become more assertive and decisive, sometimes even uncharacteristically aggressive.

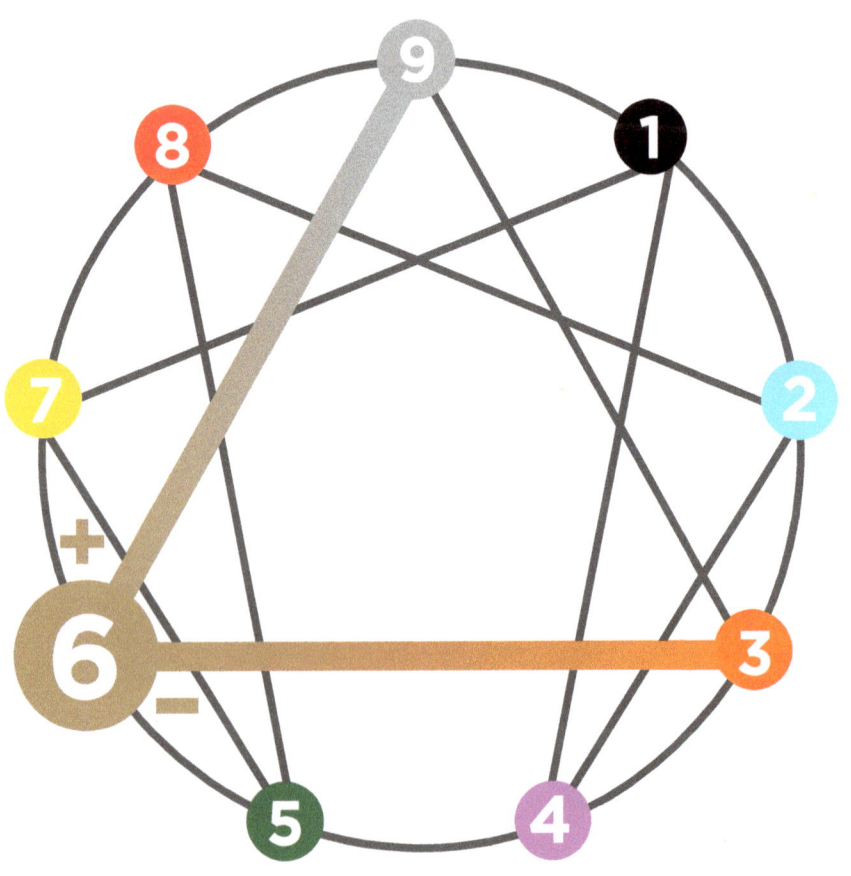

➤ Think back on a time when you weren't doing too well, or were experiencing disintegration. How did you feel like you diverted from your normal way of being? Do you see any of the aforementioned signs of disintegration in yourself?

COMPARING SELF CONSTANTLY

OVERLY EMOTIONAL

SUSPICIOUS

REACTIVE

AFRAID TO TRY NEW THINGS

CYNICAL

INSENSITIVE

NUMB ANXIETY WITH ACTIVITY

When healthy, and in seasons or moments of integration, SIXes move toward NINE and take on some of the healthier NINE traits. Their usually scattered and fearful minds become much calmer and more peaceful, not stressing about the little things that a SIX may normally stress over. They're able to stop thinking about all of the possible bad outcomes and believe that everything will be okay. When SIXes do the very thing that scares them and act in true courage, they come to a place of peace and calm because they now know from experience that the "worst" may happen, but they'll get through it. Healthy SIXes know how to truly rest and be at ease with the circumstances they can't control. They embody the safety and security they crave, becoming a safe sanctuary where others can feel understood and cared for.

➤ **Think of a time when you were healthy and integrated. It could have been a day or a more prolonged season. What positive changes did you notice? What parts of that experience do you wish would become a more normal part of your life?**

_____

_____

_____

_____

_____

_____

_____

_____

_____

_____

ENNEADICTIONARY FOR SIXES

Inner Committee (n.): SIX minds are filled with the voices and opinions of trusted people, an Inner Committee. This Inner Committee is constantly debating and speaking, influencing a SIX's thoughts and often leading to analysis paralysis.

Analysis Paralysis (n.): An inability to move forward on decisions because the SIX may not trust others' advice, nor their own thoughts or opinions.

Worst-Case Scenario (n.): SIXes have the capacity to put a negative spin on all situations. They deal with fear via pessimism and worst-case scenario planning, often invoking situations that would never even occur to other types. SIXes are always convinced that the worst is a very real possibility.

Pre-Traumatic Stress Disorder (n.): The "reliving of traumatic events" or episodes before they ever take place (if they do at all).

Testing (v.): SIXes will frequently test people in their lives, checking for loyalty and agreement as well as reassurance.

➤ Did any of these definitions particularly strike you? Is there anything that highly resonates with you?

_____

_____

_____

_____

_____

_____

➤ Is there anything you strongly disagree with? What is it? How do you experience things differently?

_____

_____

_____

_____

_____

_____

_____

➤ How does having an Inner Committee serve you? What do you hope to gain by having so many sources of input? What are you avoiding?

_____

_____

_____

_____

_____

_____

➤ What do you fear in making decisions? Do you think it's possible to analyze the situation enough? At what point would you recommend someone else in your position make the decision?

_____

_____

_____

_____

_____

_____

➤ Ask a trusted friend to tell you next time they see you doing something specifically to test them. How was that experience for you? What impact did it have on your self-awareness?

_____

_____

_____

_____

_____

➤ What are some occasions where your worst-case scenario planning was helpful to you? What about when things went way better than anticipated? How does your worst-case scenario planning keep you from actually living the life you want to live?

_____

_____

_____

_____

_____

ORIGIN STORIES/ CHILDHOOD WOUNDS

In this section, we will explore some common childhood wounds for SIXes. Please remember that these are not necessarily universal. You may relate to some aspects of a SIX's origin story very strongly, and others not at all. If your experience is different, take the time to put the specifics of your experience into words. Our aim is not to guess what sort of trauma you experienced growing up but rather to help you pinpoint how you came to have the patterns and coping mechanisms of an enneagram SIX.

Growing up, were you

- raised to believe that the world was a dangerous place due to overly protective, hovering caregivers?
- raised in a dangerous/unpredictable situation, with no safe place?
- raised to blindly trust authorities without thinking for yourself?

➤ **Does any of that resonate with you? None of it? All of it? Take some time to describe this part of your origin story.**

_____

_____

_____

_____

_____

_____

_____

_____

Because of these experiences you just described, did you learn to

- turn inward to doubt reality . . .
- reject your own instincts and inner guidance . . .
- create a brave, courageous persona . . .
- protect others from unpredictability and danger . . .

. . . so that you could

- become the expert at detecting signs to help yourself know what will happen, thus coping with unpredictability?
- prepare for challenging and scary situations by processing subtle signs in the external world?
- align yourself with a new authority figure?

➤ **Which of these tendencies did you see forming in yourself growing up? What was the reward or benefit of acting this way? What was the cost of doing the opposite?**

_____

_____

_____

_____

_____

_____

_____

➤ **Which (if any) of these statements did you believe as a child?**

- I must be safe and secure.
- I can overcome unpredictability.
- I can't trust myself.

_____

_____

_____

_____

_____

_____

➤ **Approximately how much of your SIX-ness is innate to you? How much is learned?**

_____

_____

_____

_____

_____

_____

_____

➤ What would you go back and tell yourself as a child, if you could?

_____

_____

_____

_____

_____

_____

_____

_____

PART II

DIGGING DEEPER AS A TYPE SIX

We hope that by now you have uncovered some ways that SIX-ness is showing up in you, whether in your shadow side or how you move to NINE in integration and THREE in disintegration. Maybe some of the coping strategies were uncovered in your origin story.

In this next section, we want to dig deeper into some of the nuances of SIX-ness. The color that we associate with SIXes is brown, precisely because there is more nuance to brown than any other color on the spectrum. There are quite a variety of browns in the world, from bronze to coffee to mahogany to chestnut to khaki to sand. If you look at the Enneagram subtypes, you will see that out of all of the numbers, SIXes have the most variety among the three different instincts. We see various shades of brown in nature, symbolizing the rootedness and connectedness that often characterize SIXes. The very ground that supports us, both indoors and outdoors, is often brown, much as SIXes in health provide support and stability for the people in their lives. Brown is not a loud color that draws attention to itself; rather, it adapts to any environment. This natural shade is a perfect match for SIXes who possess a natural and fierce strength, especially as they face and overcome their fears. In this section, we will unpack some of the nuances of how you are a unique and particular SIX, unlike any other SIX the world has ever seen. We will explore triads, stances, subtypes, and wings, and along the way, we will prompt you to dig deeper into what shade of SIX you are.

SHADES OF SIX

LOYAL

COMMITTED

PREPARED

FAITHFUL

STRUCTURED

COURAGEOUS

ORDERED

LEADER

FUNNY

CHARMING

CONTROLLED

SECURE

RELIABLE

HARD-WORKING

AFFECTIONATE

VIGILANT

SKEPTICAL

SUPPORTIVE

HEAD TRIAD

SIXes are in the Head Triad, meaning they take in information analytically, through their minds. Their first reaction, even if it's instantaneous, is analytical. This does not mean that SIXes can't or don't have emotional or physical responses, but their analytical response comes first. Also called the Fear Triad, all types in this triad have a unique tie to fear. While FIVEs outsource their fear and SEVENs are asleep to their fear, SIXes swim in their fear. SIXes are constantly aware of what's making them anxious or unsettled, and their minds are working overtime to account for these fears.

➤ Does this depiction of the Head Triad describe you? Is there anything that highly resonates with you?

_____

_____

_____

_____

_____

_____

➤ Is there anything you strongly disagree with? What is it? How do you experience things differently?

_____

_____

_____

_____

_____

_____

_____

➤ What would it look like for you to acknowledge your fear without drowning in it?

_____

_____

_____

_____

_____

_____

➤ Do you ever use your analytical thoughts as a way to access your feelings or your gut instincts? What is helpful to you about this pattern? How is it unhelpful?

_____

_____

_____

_____

_____

_____

Part of the SIX's relationship to fear is that they lean toward pessimism, rather than optimism, as a coping strategy. They fear that what can go wrong *will* go wrong and orient their whole lives around that notion as a means of feeling safe and secure. Assuming the worst of people and situations is a way to avoid being disappointed or let down. When circumstances do go wrong, the SIX is proven right, thus solidifying their belief that the world is unsafe and others can't be trusted. They gravitate toward fear because the act of trusting others is too scary or risky.

➤ **Do these statements resonate with you?**

_____

_____

_____

_____

➤ **Can you think of a time when you deliberately leaned into pessimism? How did that experience serve your own ego? How was it unhelpful?**

_____

_____

_____

_____

_____

_____

_____

➤ What, in particular, scares you about trusting others?

_____

_____

_____

_____

_____

_____

_____

➤ When you move into NINE-ness and experience integration, how does your experience of fear change? Pay close attention to your self-talk and note your experience here.

_____

_____

_____

_____

_____

_____

_____

_____

DEPENDENT STANCE

SIXes are in the Dependent Stance. They are oriented toward other people, being dependent on others. They find their identity outside of themselves. SIXes find their value in being able to anticipate and provide for their own needs and the needs of their loved ones. They often don't trust themselves to make decisions that best serve them and need many sources of outside input. They move toward other people as a way of filling voids that they feel within themselves.

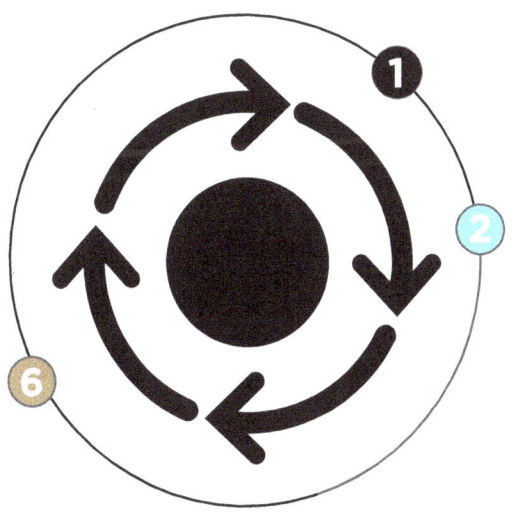

➤ Does this describe you? Is there anything that highly resonates with you?

_____

_____

_____

_____

_____

_____

➤ Is there anything you strongly disagree with? What is it? How do you experience things differently?

_____

_____

_____

_____

_____

_____

_____

➤ When was the last time you retreated away from yourself toward other people? What triggered your retreat?

_____

_____

_____

_____

_____

_____

➤ How can you tell the difference between retreating away from yourself and moving toward others out of love and care, with no ulterior motives?

_____

_____

_____

_____

_____

_____

_____

We refer to all three types in the Dependent Stance as "thinking-repressed," meaning that they do and feel more intuitively than they think. This notion may seem inconsistent with a SIX's location in the Head Triad. However, when SIXes are on autopilot, they can be quick to respond to feelings of fear or insecurity by jumping into defensive action without first stopping to think critically. It's in learning to pause and detach, before letting their worst-case scenario take over, that SIXes find their growth and integration.

➤ Have you ever had the experience of realizing that you were planning, analyzing options, or protecting others compulsively rather than thoughtfully? What did it feel like in the moment? What did it feel like afterward?

_____

_____

_____

_____

_____

➤ Has your tendency to retreat from yourself toward others ever had an impact on your relationships with those around you?

_____

_____

_____

_____

Those in the Dependent Stance also have an orientation toward the present rather than a focus on the past or the future. Their attention goes to the details right in front of them. SIXes are constantly analyzing their surroundings for threats or disturbances. Their attention to detail tends toward hypervigilance. Unaware SIXes can be reactive to what happens in front of them, rather than considering the past or future when making decisions.

➤ **When did you last find yourself being reactive? How would taking the time to think about past similar situations or future implications have served you?**

_____

_____

_____

_____

_____

➤ **What would it take for you to learn from the past, to give better context to your decisions and behaviors?**

_____

_____

_____

_____

_____

_____

WINGS

Some SIXes have a very strong wing, and some find that they have balanced wings or no wing at all. SIXes with a FIVE wing (6w5) tend to be more reserved, cautious, and cerebral. They are more likely to respond to fear or threats by dealing with them internally, with lots of thinking, researching, and analyzing. They enjoy researching all sorts of things so that they can be prepared for whatever may come their way. 6w5s are usually more introverted and withdrawn than 6w7s.

SIXes with a SEVEN wing (6w7) tend to be more outgoing, energetic, and impulsive than 6w5s. When faced with fear or the unknown, they are more likely to move right into action than a 6w5 would be. They are lively, fun, and assertive. Their minds are highly active and productive. 6w7s are more open to new experiences and endeavors when they are in places of security.

6W5   6W7

➤ Of these descriptions of 6w5 and 6w7, does one resonate more strongly with you? In what way?

_____

_____

_____

_____

_____

➤ If you have a wing, how do you find that your wing (w5, w7, or balanced) shades your SIX-ness?

_____

_____

_____

_____

_____

_____

> How does your wing balance you?

_____

_____

_____

_____

_____

_____

_____

_____

> When do you find yourself tapping into your wing? What does it provide for you?

_____

_____

_____

_____

_____

_____

_____

_____

SUBTYPES

One part of the Enneagram that unlocks a whole
lot of clarity is the nature of subtypes, or instincts.
Each person is dominant in one of three instincts:
Self-Preservation (SP), Sexual (SX), or Social (SO).
That instinct within your type is called your subtype.
Each person also has a secondary subtype and
will likely find that one of the three instincts does
not really relate to them at all. So, for example,
a SIX could be a SO/SX SIX, meaning their
dominant subtype is Social and their secondary
subtype is Sexual.

Self-Preservation (SP) SIX: SP SIXes are cautious and loyal. They are highly practical and concerned with their own security in very tangible ways. The SP SIX is what is commonly known as the "phobic" SIX, meaning that they adapt to their fears and have many ways of hedging, rather than displaying a more aggressive, combative approach. SP SIXes are the people who are always prepared for any situation. They can be more reserved and cautious than the other SIX subtypes, often taking a more subtle approach toward their circle of close people.

Sexual (SX) SIX: SX SIXes are commonly known as the "counterphobic" SIXes, meaning that while they are still motivated by fear, they take a more aggressive approach toward combating it. They are more likely to run at their fear rather than away from it. SX SIXes are the countertype, meaning they present as less SIX-ish than the other two subtypes. They are strong-willed, direct, sometimes even combative. They are bolder and more assertive than the other SIX subtypes, as well as more distrustful of people in positions of authority. They can easily mistype as an EIGHT or a ONE because their bigger personalities make them appear unafraid to confront what they see as wrong.

Social (SO) SIX: SO SIXes are a combination of phobic and counterphobic. They are dutiful, precise, and more community-minded than the other SIX subtypes. SO SIXes can see things in a very black-and-white manner, which can lead to them mistyping as ONEs. An SO SIX likes to make sure that everyone is on the same page regarding expectations. They like to have a hand in the lives of their closest people so those people will be there for them in their time of need. They are geared toward rules, order, and guidelines, because they appreciate clear expectations and reliability. SO SIXes are the people who adamantly stick to traditions among family and friends, because to them, these traditions represent closeness and stability. Unlike the SX SIX, SO SIXes can find comfort in authority figures when necessary.

➤ As you read through these subtypes, which one is your dominant type? How do you know?

_____

_____

_____

_____

_____

_____

_____

➤ Which is your secondary subtype? How do you know?

_____

_____

_____

_____

_____

_____

_____

➤ Which of these subtypes does not resonate with you?

_____

_____

_____

_____

_____

➤ Which part of the description of each subtype resonates most strongly
with you? How has your subtype shaded the sort of SIX that you are?

_____

_____

_____

_____

_____

➤ Do you see your subtype as a hindrance or a help? Why?

_____

_____

_____

_____

_____

PART III

RELATIONSHIPS
AS A TYPE SIX

YOU AND EACH TYPE

Before we talk about relationships between SIXes and each type, it's worth noting that this space is completely insufficient to fully explore this topic. Entire books have been written solely on relationships between types and how the Enneagram can affect each relationship. This table is here to help get you thinking about some potential connection points and tension points that you may encounter with each type, including fellow SIXes.

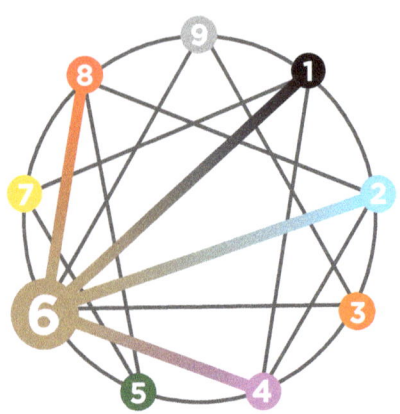

Relationship between SIX and ...	Potential places of synergy/connection	Potential places of conflict/tension
1	ONEs and SIXes are alike in so many ways, that they often mistype as each other. Their shared mental framework and commitment to others, hard work, duty, and integrity make this pair a stable and trustworthy team. At their best, each type takes the burden of responsibility off of the other's shoulders, which means these two tightly-wound types may finally find space for rest and relaxation.	At their worst, these two types can create a perfect storm, playing into each other's deepest insecurities. The ONE fears that the SIX isn't living up to their expectations, which plays into the SIX's anxieties and insecurities, which causes the SIX to withdraw, and the ONE to become more rigid, and so on and so forth. Both types need to name their mental frameworks in order to avoid this downward spiral of stress and anxiety.

Both types are in the Dependent Stance, so they place a high value on the people around them, and at their best can be stabilizing forces in the community. They will go to great lengths to make each other feel understood and cared for. They are both great at anticipating needs. TWOs and SIXes can make each other feel safe in each other's presence, which holds a high value for both types. SIXes can help TWOs discover and name what they need, while TWOs can help put SIXes at ease by also paying attention to the detailed needs of the group around them.

SIXes, especially when they are not doing well, use the people around them to ease their insecurities. TWOs can feel particularly burdened by this tendency of SIXes, as they are used to meeting the needs of others and doing whatever is necessary to make them feel cared for. Even TWOs have limits when it comes to the neediness of others. TWOs can also frustrate SIXes with their unspoken expectations. SIXes, more than most types, place a high value on knowing what is expected of them, and TWOs have a particular struggle with naming and verbalizing their expectations of people or situations.

Relationship between SIX and . . .	Potential places of synergy/connection	Potential places of conflict/tension
3	Both types are dutiful, reliable, and care a lot about being seen and trusted by the people close to them. These types offer immense help to each other in very specific ways. At their best, the THREE can help the SIX dream way bigger than they would on their own and help the SIX think through their path to success or to achieve what they would be too scared to do on their own. SIXes in health embody the safe place that THREEs need to be truly seen as they are, where it's okay to fail and to come across as flawed. THREEs need the grounding and relentless loyalty of SIXes to work through their own insecurities to truly thrive. They both understand each other as people who spend a lot of time conforming to the expectations and desires of others.	THREEs on autopilot can easily come across as shallow, impulsive people who are easily influenced in the wrong direction. Their motivation is not trustworthy at all to a SIX, which would make it a challenge to build any sort of meaningful relationship. SIXes, meanwhile, can limit themselves with their preference for the familiar, which forward-thinking and ambitious THREEs can find stunting. THREEs like to feel competent, and already struggle with what other people think about them, so when SIXes meet THREEs with skepticism and/or hovering tendencies, THREEs can feel unimportant or distrusted, or as if their competencey is being questioned.
	Both FOURs and SIXes are deeply spiritual, very sensitive, and insecure types. Both types find fascination in the shadow self and the darker parts of life. On a fun note, both types are drawn to dark stories like true crime and may enjoy watching these types of movies and shows together. Even though FOURs are not Dependent types, they are such natural relationship-builders that they will appeal to the SIX's sense of being needed and wanted in relationship. This is a strong pair that will give each other space to work through their issues without flinching or withdrawing.	Both FOURs and SIXes are rebellious types, and they can appear self-contradictory at times. Both types can easily fall into anxiousness, often around the state of their relationship: the FOUR anxious that they will not be fully seen, the SIX anxious that they will be abandoned. The hot and cold tendencies of FOURs is something that SIXes have also been known to employ, as a defense mechanism against abandonment. On the flip side, these types may also find themselves so fearful of abandonment that they actually become codependent.

Relationship between SIX and ...	Potential places of synergy/connection	Potential places of conflict/tension
5	Both types are in the Head Triad; they love to think things through, and take a more cautious approach to life. SIXes would thus see FIVEs as safe and trustworthy people who are responsible, and FIVEs would see SIXes as people who know what they're talking about and who also consider all angles. In health, both types would see the other as steady, thoughtful people who have similar approaches to life. They both love to research and be as informed as possible. SIXes can help FIVEs put their ideas into action, and FIVEs can help reason with a SIX's fears or insecurities, as there's a good chance that FIVEs have also put a lot of thought into the things that the SIX is overanalyzing.	SIXes, being in the Dependent Stance, can have very high expectations of other people to help them feel safe and secure. FIVEs, meanwhile, have a very strong distaste for unspoken expectations, and they really don't like when people put expectations on them that are either too high or too draining. On the other hand, FIVEs tend to withdraw from others when they are stressed or on autopilot, while SIXes may move toward others. A SIX may interpret the FIVE's withdrawing tendency as being unreliable in times of need.
	Two SIXes in healthy places can really understand each other like no other type can. The presence of another SIX can be calming for SIXes, as they see someone else who has similar fears, worries, or anxieties, but has overcome them to get where they are. They can also rest in knowing that they are not the only ones who are vigilant about the safety of the group as a whole, so they can relax a bit more than they otherwise would. With their high value for honesty and loyalty, their posture toward each other will put each SIX at ease and allow them to live more freely.	SIXes who are not on the same page about what is important or what is expected of each other can majorly clash. SIXes on autopilot can have very high and/or specific expectations of people and situations, and if those expectations go unspoken, the two types can easily wind up on very different pages and thus not trust each other's motives at all. SIXes on autopilot can also be territorial, so if one steps into the other's circle to assert help or control, the other SIX will not respond well.

Relationship between SIX and ...	Potential places of synergy/connection	Potential places of conflict/tension
7	As two types in the Head Triad, SIXes and SEVENs tend to find each other in the world. The naturally optimistic SEVEN provides great balance and perspective for the naturally pessimistic SIX. SEVENs dream up fantastic new worlds, and SIXes help build them. SIXes provide practical information about the very real fears that SEVENs usually reframe. SEVENs help SIXes lighten up with when the fear gets too crushing.	When these two types are in disintegration, their opposite reactions to fear can cause a rift between them. SEVENs migrate to the future as a part of the Aggressive Stance, and SIXes remain in the present moment, as a part of the Dependent Stance. SIXes can be very mentally rigid and inflexible, living a life of self-imposed rules and limits, while SEVENs do their best to eliminate all rules and limits.
	SIXes and EIGHTs share a general protectiveness of people who are close to them and a mistrust of authority figures who they have not vetted. They understand each other well because of that shared posture. EIGHTs are generally very consistent people who don't have time for sugar-coating anything, so a SIX would appreciate that they never have to guess what an EIGHT is really thinking. SIXes are very loyal people who have high values for honesty, so an EIGHT would appreciate that a SIX would be honest and forthcoming with them, especially when there is already a good foundation to the relationship. These types can make a really great pair, in work, friendship, or romance, as an EIGHT would push toward places a SIX might be too apprehensive to go, and a SIX would cover a lot of bases that an EIGHT would miss with their tendency to act very quickly.	SIXes can be slow to act and make decisions, which is usually frustrating to EIGHTs. SIXes also have a tendency to ask questions repeatedly or do things to test the loyalty or reliability of loved ones, which EIGHTs would have little patience for. On the other hand, EIGHTs can tend to live life with an "act, then think" posture, which SIXes could can see as impulsive and untrustworthy. Many EIGHTs are seen as a little rough around the edges, so an EIGHT's bluntness or other behavior that others see as "inappropriate" could break trust with a SIX who doesn't know the EIGHT that well. SIXes are also one of the more sensitive types, so the perceived aggression from an EIGHT could make a relationship challenging. Both types are quick to deem others as incompetent or untrustworthy, so it can take a long time for these two to warm up to each other.

NINEs and SIXes often gravitate toward each other. NINEs exude the calm that SIXes long for, and SIXes can help bring NINEs into the present moment with their hypervigilance. SIXes make NINEs feel cared for, and they pay attention to things that NINEs wouldn't pay attention to for themselves. All three types in the Anchor Triad (THREE, SIX, and NINE) are used to conforming to the world around them, so they can easily meet the needs of the other. Both types are in the middle of their triads and are used to straddling fences.

If they are unhealthy or unaware, both types have tendencies to rely heavily on the other. NINEs merge with other people and forget themselves in the process, and SIXes so deeply embed people into their own security blankets, that if there is a disruption in that system, then they themselves are no longer "okay." They can both lose themselves in the process. In stress, the hypervigilance of the SIX and the apparent lack of vigilance from the NINE can easily rub each other the wrong way.

➤ As you read through these relationship prompts, can you think of any relationships in which you may be misunderstanding each other? How can you connect better?

_____

_____

_____

_____

➤ Does this give language to any places of conflict that you're experiencing with another person? How do you think the Enneagram explains this particular tension?

_____

_____

_____

_____

➤ Are there people of a certain type in your life whom you don't "get"? How can your relationship grow from better understanding this dynamic?

_____

_____

_____

_____

RIPPLE EFFECTS

As we say in our first book, *What's Your Enneatype?*, your actions and tendencies affect more people than just you. It's better for everyone when you pay attention to the influence of your actions. These questions are designed to help you think about and become more aware of the ripple effects of your SIX-ish behaviors.

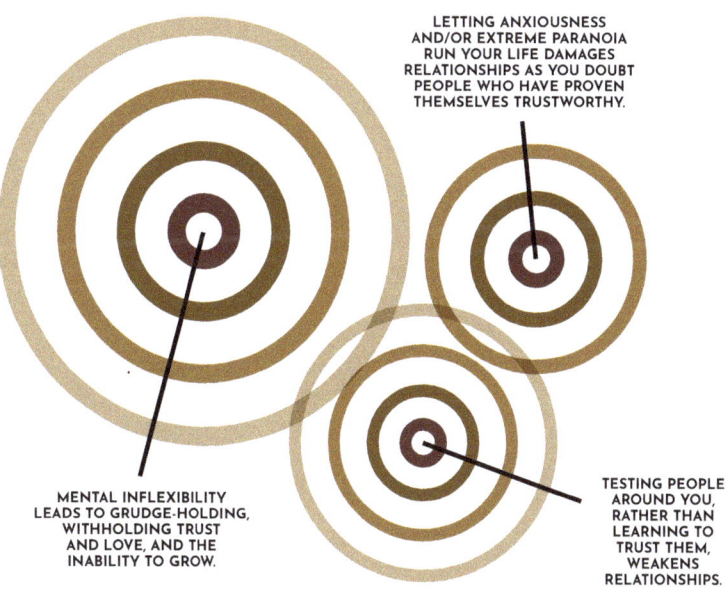

LETTING ANXIOUSNESS AND/OR EXTREME PARANOIA RUN YOUR LIFE DAMAGES RELATIONSHIPS AS YOU DOUBT PEOPLE WHO HAVE PROVEN THEMSELVES TRUSTWORTHY.

MENTAL INFLEXIBILITY LEADS TO GRUDGE-HOLDING, WITHHOLDING TRUST AND LOVE, AND THE INABILITY TO GROW.

TESTING PEOPLE AROUND YOU, RATHER THAN LEARNING TO TRUST THEM, WEAKENS RELATIONSHIPS.

➤ Have there been any situations recently in which you tested a person's trust too many times, and it ended up causing a rift in the relationship? What was your thought process in the moment? What was your thought process afterward?

_____

_____

_____

_____

➤ How do others feel when you project your doubts and insecurities on them? How does that make you feel?

_____

_____

_____

_____

➤ What are some past hurts or grievances that you've been holding on to for too long? How does holding onto them benefit you? How does it cost you?

_____

_____

_____

_____

➤ Can you think of a relationship or a situation in which you're constantly expecting the other person to let you down? Is that fair? How does the expectation of failure limit both you and the other person involved?

_____

_____

_____

➤ Think of a time when you had very high expectations of someone or something that you never expressed. What was the breaking point? How would things have been different if you had been honest about your expectations with others? With yourself?

_____

_____

_____

➤ Think of a time when you raised a valid concern that others truly benefitted from. Now think of a time where you were simply projecting an insecurity on anyone who would listen. What would be the cost of learning the difference between valid concerns and projecting insecurities? How do others pay the cost when you project your insecurities?

_____

_____

_____

PART IV

THE WAY FORWARD AS A TYPE SIX

This final section will help you find a way forward. We believe that the goal of a tool like the Enneagram is not to put you in a box but to help you identify the box you have been living in and find a way out. We hope the first three sections of this workbook have helped you identify what that box looks like, and it is our objective that this final section will help you map out the way forward: to unlearn the box of SIX, to move beyond the labels, and find your way into a flourishing life unencumbered by the burdens of people-pleasing and self-neglect, full of true, rooted generosity and hospitality.

FALSE SELF/TRUE SELF

Earlier in this guide, we walked you through your SIX origin story: how did you become a SIX? What caused you to learn SIX-ness? In this section, we want to dig deeper into your False Self to uncover your True Self. We will examine your autopilot behaviors, coping strategies, and reactions to your fears and insecurities—all the things that form the basis of your False Self.

A SIX's False Self often sounds like this:

➤ "If people aren't regularly reaffirming our relationship, they don't care about me."

➤ "Nobody wants to hear what I have to say."

➤ "I'm capable of protecting all of my loved ones from all harm or danger. I can control this."

➤ "If it can go wrong, it will go wrong."

➤ "I need to hold things together."

➤ "I cannot trust myself or others."

➤ Which of these quotes from the SIX's False Self sounds most familiar to you?

_____

_____

_____

_____

_____

_____

_____

➤ Are there any that do not resonate with you?

_____

_____

_____

_____

_____

_____

_____

_____

Spend some time challenging your False Self by asking these questions, and write down your responses below.

➤ **What could happen if you trusted that your people have your best interests at heart? What can be gained from not always testing your relationships?**

_____

_____

_____

_____

_____

_____

➤ **What do others miss out on when you assume that they don't want to hear what you have to say?**

_____

_____

_____

_____

_____

_____

_____

➤ How do your attempts to protect everyone from harm serve your ego? What would happen if you can't help them?

_____

_____

_____

_____

_____

_____

➤ What do you miss out on by always planning for the worst? What would change if you had your eyes on the best case?

_____

_____

_____

_____

_____

_____

_____

➤ What does your hypervigilance cost you? What does it cost those around you?

_____

_____

_____

_____

_____

_____

➤ What would happen if your loved ones didn't need you to anticipate everything that could go wrong? What would happen if you loved them as they want to be loved?

_____

_____

_____

_____

_____

_____

> How can you tell when you're operating out of your False Self?

_____

_____

_____

_____

_____

_____

_____

_____

_____

UNLEARNING

As you unpack what your unique shade of SIX looks like, you will likely uncover some of the beautiful, life-giving, flourishing aspects of what it means to be a SIX. Spend some time reviewing your answers in this guide, then reflect on the following pages.

➤ What is your favorite part of being a SIX? What aspect of being a type SIX is most life-giving?

_____

_____

_____

_____

_____

_____

➤ What is the biggest gift of SIX-ness? Ask this same question of some of your closest people and write their answers below as well.

_____

_____

_____

_____

_____

_____

_____

Likewise, you have probably identified some aspects of SIX-ness that are unhealthy behaviors and coping strategies. These things are no longer serving you and need to be unlearned.

➤ **What aspect of your SIX-ness is unhealthy and needs to be unlearned?**

_____

_____

_____

_____

_____

_____

➤ **What would change if you unlearned these things?**

_____

_____

_____

_____

_____

_____

_____

➤ What is the next positive step for you in unlearning these things?

_____

_____

_____

_____

_____

_____

_____

_____

_____

PURPOSEFUL PRACTICES

Sometimes the process of unlearning is easier when you have disciplines, rhythms, and practices to help you. Below are some suggestions for you as you work on unlearning the shadow side of SIX and begin to silence the False Self.

Memorials: As people who are always scanning the horizon for what could go wrong, it's important for SIXes to have very tangible reminders of what has happened in the past and how they overcame difficulties. You are strong and resilient, and many of you have faced a lot of struggles to get to where you are now. Having some sort of memorial (it could be a token of sorts, a picture, or something you hang on your wall) to remind you of what you have been through and how you overcame can serve you in the future as you face whatever comes your way.

Mantras: In a similar vein, having mantras or phrases that you can repeat to yourself over and over again can help center and ground you in what you know to be true, rather than what your fear or insecurity may be telling you. This process will look different for every SIX, but finding a phrase you know to be true and committing it to memory will help shape your thoughts whenever those red flags come up and fear starts to rise. This practice can help you see your fear for what it is, rather than allowing fear to control you.

Self-Examination: Asking yourself hard questions when fears arise will also challenge your thinking and cause you to stop and reflect before you react. You can keep the worries and worst-case scenario planning at bay by responding to red flags with questions. Is this really true? Is it likely to happen? Do I need to be the one to fix it? Asking these questions is another important step in observing your own fears and worries rather than letting your life become dictated by them.

Take Deep Breaths: Types in the Dependent Stance feel and act more than they stop and think. Make a habit of stopping to take some deep breaths to let your mind catch up to your heart when you feel unsafe, when you see a need, or when you feel threatened.

Practice Courage: You don't need to be jumping off cliffs or speaking in front of thousands of people to practice courage. Courage is overcoming your fears and doing whatever it is that scares you. Make a practice of regularly (whether it be weekly, biweekly, monthly, etc.) and consciously choosing to do the thing that you're scared of. Invite a trusted friend into the process and have them hold you accountable. Fear does not need to have the final say; you can exert control over your fear.

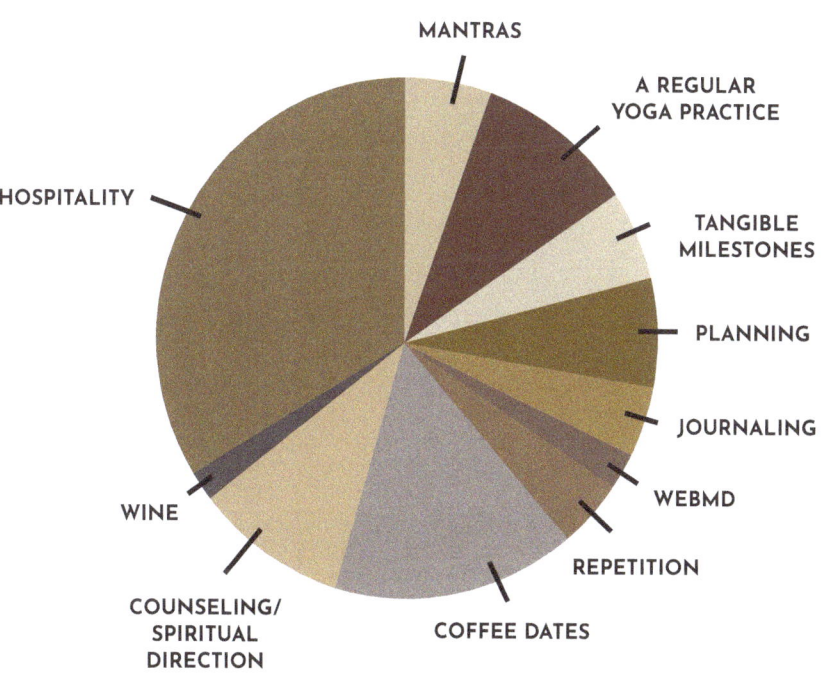

MANTRAS

A REGULAR
YOGA PRACTICE

TANGIBLE
MILESTONES

PLANNING

JOURNALING

WEBMD

REPETITION

COFFEE DATES

COUNSELING/
SPIRITUAL
DIRECTION

WINE

HOSPITALITY

➤ Which of the previously listed practices are you already engaging with?

_____

_____

_____

_____

_____

_____

➤ Which of the previously listed practices sounds most challenging to you? Why do you think that is?

_____

_____

_____

_____

_____

_____

_____

➤ What is a practice that can get you out of your head and into your body and your heart? How does it serve you as a whole person?

_____

_____

_____

_____

_____

_____

➤ Is there one practice, or perhaps something that is not previously listed, that you want to implement this week? What steps do you need to take to make that happen?

_____

_____

_____

_____

_____

_____

_____

_____

BODY

SELF-DESTRUCTIVE/HYSTERICAL   EVASIVE/HIGHLY REACTIVE/   HARD-WORKING/STABLE/SECURE
UNPREDICTABLE

MIND

IRRATIONAL/FEEL PERSECUTED   ANXIOUS/VIGILANT/INDECISIVE   POSITIVE/CREATE STABILITY

HEART

PANICKY/FEELINGS   MOODY/HYPERSENSITIVE   SENSITIVE/EMOTIONALLY
OF INFERIORITY   HONEST

SELF

ASHAMED/SELF-HATE   SUSPICIOUS OF SELF/   COURAGEOUS/INDEPENDENT/
BEGIN TO LOOK FOR ALLIANCES   SELF-AFFIRMING

OTHERS

DIVISIVE/ BELLIGERENT   PASSIVE-AGGRESSIVE/   TRUSTING/INTERDEPENDENT/
"FRIEND OR FOE" BEHAVIOR   COMMUNAL

JUST FOR FUN!

FEARFUL OF   FEARFUL OF   FEARFUL OF
EVERYTHING + EVERYONE   BEAR ATTACKS   CLEAR + PRESENT DANGER

YOUR NEXT STEPS

As this guide comes to an end, we hope that you spend some time reflecting on what your next steps need to be. SIXes who don't address their unhealthy patterns and habits can end up walking down a very dangerous road. It can look like testing other people constantly until it hinders your relationship. It could look like investing so much in worst-case scenario planning that you miss the life that's happening right in front of you. It could look like hovering and clinging so tightly to your loved ones in the name of "protecting" them that it actually drives them away. Living by mere impulses is costly, both to you and the people around you.

We are proud of you for taking steps toward unlearning the aspects of SIX-ness that are harmful and boldly expressing the aspects of SIX-ness that are a gift to the world. This requires a lot of hard work, self-awareness, and humility. It requires listening to your gut and actually following your intuition rather than spiraling into further analysis paralysis. It requires challenging your own internal narratives, regardless of how loud or persistent they may be. It requires rising above your fear and doing what the situation requires.

Each day, you will be faced with a choice: to continue your unconscious patterns or to step away from them toward courage, true connection, and peace. The more you incorporate these practices, the more you will find yourself caring for yourself and your loved ones out of a place of rootedness and true security, rather than trying to overcompensate for your fears and projecting onto others. The more you engage in this work, the more you will embody and become the safe haven for others that you long for yourself. Your care, support, and loyalty for others, free from fear, is truly one of the greatest gifts you can offer to the world.

Lift your head, dear SIX. See how far you've already come.

— Liz and Josh

NOTES

ABOUT THE AUTHORS

Liz Carver and **Josh Green** run one of the most popular Enneagram accounts on social media, **@justmyenneatype**. Liz is the creative director at Eastbrook Church in Wisconsin, and Josh is a campus minister for InterVarsity Christian Fellowship. Together, they wrote *What's Your Enneatype?* Visit their website **myenneatype.com** for more information.

What's Your Enneatype?
978-1-5923-3952-5

INDEX

A

analysis paralysis
    definition of, 27–28
    hyper-vigilance as, 50
    origins of, 29

C

childhood wounds
    beliefs, 34
    developed tendencies, 33
    safety and, 32
    variety of, 31
color, characteristics of,
    38–39

D

Dependent Stance
    description of, 45–46
    expectations and, 63
    retreating, 47, 49
    "thinking-repressed," 49
    presence of mind, 50, 84
    rigidity of, 64
    TWOs and, 61
disintegration
    safety and, 21
    SEVENs and, 64
    THREEs and, 21
    warning signs, 23–25

E

EIGHTs
    mistyping as, 55
    relationships with, 64
    testing and, 64
Enneadictionary

analysis paralysis,
    27–28, 29
Inner Committee, 27–29
pre-traumatic stress
    disorder, 27–28
testing, 27–28, 30
worst-cast scenario,
    27–28, 30

F

False Self
    challenge questions,
        75–78
    hyper-vigilance and,
        76–77
    recognizing, 78
    relationships and, 73,
        75, 76
    testing, 75
    voice of, 73–74
fear
    acknowledgment of, 42
    acting against, 19, 26
    control of, 19, 84
    FIVE wings, 51
    Head Triad and, 40,
        42, 49
    hyper-vigilance and, 16,
        20, 27, 29, 50, 76–77
    integration and, 26,
        44, 49
    manifestation of, 17–18
    mantras for, 84
    pessimism and, 43–44
    settling for security, 18
    SEVEN wings, 51
    shadow side and, 16–19

subtypes and, 55
    "thinking-repressed," 49
FIVEs
    Head Triad and, 63
    relationships with, 63
    wings and, 51–52
FOURs, relationships
    with, 62

H

Head Triad
    description of, 40–41
    fear and, 40, 42, 49
    FIVEs and, 63
    pessimism and, 43–44

I

Inner Committee
    benefits of, 29
    definition of, 27–29
integration
    detachment and, 49
    fear and, 44
    NINEs and, 26, 44

M

motivation
    "counterphobic," 55
    ego and, 15
    security as, 13–14
    THREEs and, 62
    verbalizing, 15

N

NINEs
    integration and, 26, 44
    relationships with, 65

O

ONEs
  mistyping as, 55
  relationships with, 61
origin stories
  beliefs, 34
  developed tendencies, 33
  safety and, 32
  trust and, 32, 34
  variety of, 31

P

pre-traumatic stress
  disorder, 27-28
purposeful practices
  breathing, 84
  courage, 84
  mantras, 84
  memorials, 84
  self-examination, 84

R

relationships
  ONEs, 61
  TWOs, 61
  THREEs, 62
  FOURs, 62
  FIVEs, 63
  SIXes, 63
  SEVENs, 64
  EIGHTs, 64
  NINEs, 65
  conflict in, 66
  expectations in, 43,
    63, 69
  False Self and, 73,
    75, 76
  hyper-vigilance in, 76-77
  misunderstandings, 66
  NINEs and, 65
  retreating from, 49
  rigidity in, 64
  safety and, 13
  testing, 27-28, 30, 68
  trust and, 62, 75
ripple effects
  expectations of
    failure, 69
  grievances, 68
  projection, 68, 69
  testing, 68
  Worst-Case Scenario, 68

S

safety
  acting against fear,
    19, 26
  disintegration and, 21
  expectations and, 43
  integration and, 26
  as motivation, 13
  origin stories and, 32, 34
  relationships and, 13
  settling for, 18
  shadow side and, 18
  vigilance and, 20
self check-in, 88
SEVENs
  disintegration, 64
  relationships and, 64
  wings, 51-52
shadow side
  description of, 16-17
  fear and, 16-19
subtypes
  as benefit, 57
  color and, 38
  dominant subtype,
    54, 56
  as hinderance, 57
  secondary subtype,
    54, 56
  Self-Preservation (SP),
    55-57
  Sexual (SX), 55-57
  Social (SO), 55-57

T

testing
  acknowledgement of, 30
  conflict from, 68
  definition of, 27-28
  EIGHTs and, 64
  False Self and, 75
THREEs
  disintegration and, 21
  motivation and, 62
  relationships with, 62
  trust and, 62
trust
  authority figures, 55, 64
  expectations and, 43, 44
  as motivation, 13
  Inner Committee, 27
  origin stories and, 32, 34
  relationships and, 62, 75
  ripple effects, 68
TWOs
  Dependent Stance
    and, 61
  relationships with, 61

U

unlearning, 79-82

W

wings
  balance from, 53
  benefits of, 53
  FIVEs, 51-52
  SEVENs, 51-52
worst-case scenario
  definition of, 27-28
  detachment from, 49
  as benefit, 30
  confronting, 16
  as hinderance, 30
  ripple effects, 68
  self-examination and, 84

CPSIA information can be obtained
at www.ICGtesting.com
Printed in the USA
LVHW071149230322
714187LV00019B/683

9 780760 377819